Who Was
Winston Churchill?

Who Was Winston Churchill?

By Ellen Labrecque

Illustrated by Jerry Hoare

Grosset & Dunlap
An Imprint of Penguin Group (USA) LLC

To Sam and Juliet Labrecque—EL

GROSSET & DUNLAP
Published by the Penguin Group
Penguin Group (USA) LLC, 375 Hudson Street, New York, New York 10014, USA

USA | Canada | UK | Ireland | Australia | New Zealand | India | South Africa | China

penguin.com
A Penguin Random House Company

Text copyright © 2015 by Ellen Labrecque. Illustrations copyright © 2015 by Penguin Group (USA) LLC. All rights reserved. Published by Grosset & Dunlap, a division of Penguin Young Readers Group, 345 Hudson Street, New York, New York 10014. GROSSET & DUNLAP is a trademark of Penguin Group (USA) LLC. Printed in the USA.

Library of Congress Cataloging-in-Publication Data is available.

ISBN 978-0-448-48300-9   10 9 8 7 6 5 4 3 2 1

Contents

Who Was Winston Churchill?

When Winston Churchill walked into the House of Commons to make his first speech as prime minister of England, he was sixty-five years old. He wore a dark suit and a serious face.

It was May 13, 1940, and the beginning of World War II, the deadliest war in history. When Winston entered the giant hall, the six hundred Members of Parliament did not applaud. They sat silently. Many of them doubted that England could survive the war. Many wanted to make peace with Adolf Hitler of Germany.

"You ask, what is our aim?" Winston boomed into the microphone. "I can answer in one word. It is victory. Victory at all costs. Victory in spite of all terror. Victory however long and hard the road may be. For without victory there is no survival."

The speech was short, but electrifying. When he finished, thunderous applause rose from the crowd. Winston's powerful words made his audience feel hopeful.

Winston Churchill was a master public speaker and writer. As World War II raged on, Winston made many speeches that rallied his people. His voice was broadcast on the radio around the world.

He gave people courage during the dark days of
the war.

Winston lived for ninety years as a soldier, politician, writer, and painter. He endured many failures and setbacks during his long life. But, when he was needed the most, he rose to the challenge. Winston Churchill was the right man, at the right time.

Chapter 1
A Royal Childhood

Winston Churchill was born two months before his due date on November 30, 1874. Perhaps he was in a hurry to begin his remarkable life! After all, he was the firstborn child to one of the most rich and famous families in England.

Winston's family home was called Blenheim Palace in Woodstock, England. It had 187 rooms and sat on two thousand acres!

Queen Victoria ruled England when Winston was born. During her reign, from 1837 to 1901, Great Britain was the most powerful country in the world. The Churchill family was part of the British aristocracy,

QUEEN VICTORIA

or the country's wealthy ruling class. Winston was a member of one of a few hundred British families who held most of the land, money, and power.

Winston's father, Lord Randolph Churchill, came from a long line of British nobility. Lord Randolph's father—Winston's grandfather, John Spencer-Churchill—was the seventh Duke of Marlborough. From the day he was born,

Winston was taught that Great Britain was the greatest country on earth.

"I was a child of the Victorian era," Winston wrote. "When the realization of the greatness of our empire and of our duty to preserve it was ever growing stronger."

THE FIRST GREAT CHURCHILL

WINSTON CHURCHILL'S FAMILY HISTORY DATES BACK TO THE 1600S. JOHN CHURCHILL, WHO WAS BORN IN 1650, WAS AWARDED THE TITLE DUKE OF MARLBOROUGH.

JOHN WAS ONE OF ENGLAND'S GREATEST GENERALS. HE LED GREAT BRITAIN TO VICTORY IN BATTLES AGAINST FRANCE IN THE EIGHTEENTH CENTURY. AS A REWARD, THE ROYAL FAMILY HELPED GET HIM THE LAND TO BUILD BLENHEIM PALACE.

SINCE JOHN, TEN MORE CHURCHILLS HAVE BEEN CALLED DUKE OF MARLBOROUGH. THE TITLE IS PASSED DOWN TO THE FIRSTBORN OF THE FAMILY. BECAUSE WINSTON'S GRANDFATHER WAS THE SEVENTH DUKE, HIS FIRSTBORN SON, GEORGE SPENCER-CHURCHILL—WINSTON'S UNCLE—WAS THE EIGHTH DUKE. WINSTON'S FATHER WAS THE THIRD-BORN SON IN HIS FAMILY, SO HE WAS NOT GIVEN THE TITLE. THE ELEVENTH DUKE, JOHN SPENCER-CHURCHILL, IS A DISTANT COUSIN OF WINSTON'S. HE CURRENTLY LIVES PART OF THE YEAR IN BLENHEIM PALACE, WHERE WINSTON WAS BORN.

Winston's mother, Jeanette (Jennie) Jerome, was a beautiful and wealthy American. Jennie's family was in England on vacation when she met Lord Randolph. They became engaged just days after they met.

Winston's mother and father loved their son. But, like most wealthy English parents at the time, they did not spend much time with him. Instead, Randolph spent his days working for the British government. Jennie spent her days going to parties.

As an adult, Winston wrote that his mother "shone for me like the evening star. I loved her dearly, but at a distance."

Winston was raised and adored by his nanny, Mrs. Elizabeth Everest. He called her "Woomany." Woomany looked after Winston for his entire childhood. She cared for him all day and tucked him into bed at night.

When Winston was two, the Churchills moved to Dublin, Ireland. Winston's grandfather became an official for the British government there. Winston's father went to work for him as his personal secretary.

Winston was a lonely child and had few playmates. But he loved playing with his toy soldiers in his family's garden. He fought pretend battles and made forts for the soldiers in the dirt.

Winston's only sibling, his brother, John (Jack) Stranger Spencer-Churchill, was born when Winston was five years old. He and Jack were good friends their entire lives. Soon after Jack was born,

Lord Randolph started a new job in the British government. The Churchills moved back to London.

Like many wealthy English boys, Winston was sent to boarding school when he was seven. He attended St. George's School in Ascot, England. The headmaster at St. George's was a strict man who beat the boys if they misbehaved.

"How I hated this school," Winston said. "I counted the days and hours to the end of every term."

Winston missed his brother, Jack. He also hated most of his subjects, especially math. He loved to escape by reading books. One of his favorites was *Treasure*  *Island* by Robert Louis Stevenson, a story about pirates searching for gold. Winston dreamed of having his own adventures someday.

When Winston was twelve, he was enrolled at the Harrow School. It was one of the most well-known boys schools in England. Before Winston arrived, six graduates of the school had already gone on to become prime minister—the political leader—of England.

Winston spent four years at Harrow. He was a poor student in science and math, but he was a gifted writer. He could also memorize long poems. His favorite poem was *Lays of Ancient Rome* by Lord Macaulay. The poem was 1,200 lines about heroes and death in battle. He recited the poem with emotion, like a great actor. Winston also became the fencing champion at Harrow. He loved waging "battles," fighting with swords against his fencing opponents.

Winston wrote many letters to his parents while at boarding school. They wrote to him as well, but rarely visited. Instead, Winston's former nanny, Mrs. Everest, visited him at Harrow. She also visited Jack, who was at a different boarding school at the time.

After Harrow, Winston joined the military. He loved the idea of becoming a soldier. Winston took the entrance exam for the Royal Military Academy at Sandhurst, a training center for future British officers. He failed twice. But Winston never gave up. He finally passed on his third try. It was September 1893, and Winston was nineteen years old. He couldn't wait to fight for his beloved Great Britain.

Chapter 2
Soldier and Writer

Winston Churchill spent fifteen months at the Royal Military Academy at Sandhurst. He learned how to ride horses and how to lead soldiers in battle. Now that he was learning about something he loved, he excelled. Winston graduated in December 1894. He ranked eighth of the 150 students in his class.

As Winston's career was beginning, his father's life was ending. Lord Randolph had been sick for years. He died on January 24, 1895. He was forty-five years old. Winston was sad about his father's death. But he was crushed when his beloved nanny, Mrs. Everest, died later that same year. Home on leave from the army, Winston was at her bedside when she passed away. "She had been my dearest and most intimate friend during the whole of the twenty years I had lived," Winston wrote about her.

After Sandhurst, Winston was made a second
lieutenant in the cavalry. The cavalry was a
section of the army that fought on horseback.
He spent six months in training. But Winston
wanted to see real fighting. In November 1895, he
traveled to Cuba as a reporter covering the Cuban
War of Independence. He had a deal with a
London newspaper, the *Daily Graphic*. He was to
write articles for them describing his adventures.

While in Cuba, Winston formed his lifelong love of Cuban cigars. Later in his life, he was frequently seen with one clenched between his teeth.

After Cuba, Winston was sent with his regiment to Bangalore, India. Great Britain had ruled India since 1858.

They kept an army station in the hills of Bangalore to protect their land and the people. At first, Winston had a lot of free time. He used it to read books and write stories about his adventures. But during his nearly three years in India, he was also called to fight in two wars against the Indian people who wanted to be free from British rule. Winston helped squash both of these rebellions.

Winston left India in March 1899. Later that same year, he went to South Africa to fight in the Boer War. The war was a struggle between the British and the Dutch-speaking settlers, the Boers. The Boers wanted to rule South Africa, and so did the British.

During one of the South African battles, Winston helped rescue a British train that had been ambushed by Boer soldiers. He was captured and taken as a prisoner of war in Pretoria, South Africa. He spent his twenty-fifth birthday locked up. Eventually, Winston escaped through a bathroom window. After newspapers reported on his daring prison escape, Winston became famous back home in Great Britain.

THE BRITISH EMPIRE

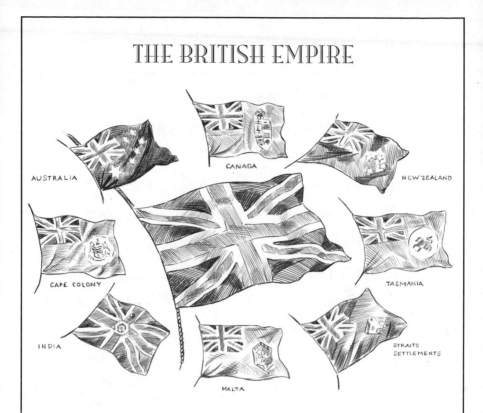

DURING THE VICTORIAN ERA, THE REIGN OF QUEEN VICTORIA (1837–1901), THE BRITISH EMPIRE REACHED ITS GREATEST HEIGHTS. BY THE DAWN OF THE TWENTIETH CENTURY, IT HAD GROWN TO ENCOMPASS ONE-QUARTER OF THE EARTH'S LANDMASS, INCLUDING A POPULATION OF FOUR HUNDRED MILLION PEOPLE. IT WAS CALLED "THE EMPIRE ON WHICH THE SUN NEVER SETS." DURING THIS TIME, GREAT BRITAIN RULED ALL OF CANADA, INDIA, AND AUSTRALIA, AS WELL AS MANY COUNTRIES IN AFRICA.

Chapter 3
Young Statesman

Winston was back in England by the fall of 1900. As a war hero, he knew it was a good time to become involved with politics. Winston didn't want to wait to be appointed to a government position by the queen. He wanted to earn a position by being elected by the British people. Winston ran for a seat in the British Parliament and won. After

the election, he went on a speaking tour across Britain, the United States, and Canada. Winston earned quite a bit of money speaking about his South African adventures during the Boer War.

KING EDWARD VII

Winston's first parliamentary term began in February 1901. Queen Victoria had died the previous month. Winston was now serving under King Edward VII, Queen Victoria's eldest son. Winston remained in the House of Commons as an elected official for most of the next sixty-three years. He would serve four kings and one queen, Elizabeth II.

Members of Parliament were either part of the Liberal Party, the Labour Party, or the Conservative Party. At first, Winston was a member of the Conservative Party. The Conservative Party worked mostly for what wealthy upper-class people wanted. The Liberal and Labour Parties were more concerned with the needs of the working class and the poor.

PARLIAMENT AND THE PRIME MINISTER

PARLIAMENT IS THE GROUP OF POLITICIANS THAT MAKES AND PASSES LAWS IN GREAT BRITAIN. THE BRITISH PARLIAMENT IS MADE UP OF THE HOUSE OF LORDS AND THE HOUSE OF COMMONS. THE MEMBERS OF THE HOUSE OF LORDS ARE APPOINTED, INCLUDING SOME BY THE MONARCH (THE KING OR QUEEN). THE MEMBERS OF THE HOUSE OF COMMONS ARE ELECTED BY THE CITIZENS OF THE UNITED KINGDOM.

THE PRIME MINISTER (PM) IS A MEMBER OF
THE HOUSE OF COMMONS AND IS THE MOST
IMPORTANT POLITICIAN IN GREAT BRITAIN. HE OR
SHE IS THE LEADER OF THE PARTY IN POWER. THE
PRIME MINISTER APPOINTS CABINET MINISTERS,
HELPS CREATE GOVERNMENT POLICY, AND MEETS
REGULARLY WITH THE KING OR QUEEN TO GIVE
AND RECEIVE ADVICE.

Winston made his first speech to the members of the house four days after his term began. Usually, Members of Parliament waited a lot longer to make their first speech. But Winston,

who loved speaking in public, couldn't resist.
He always spoke slowly and had a rough voice. He
spoke about the Boer War in South Africa, which
was still raging. The speech was a big success.

Winston soon discovered he disagreed with other members of the Conservative Party. He passionately believed in helping the working class and the poor. The Conservative Party wasn't concerned with this. In 1904, he switched to the Liberal Party. The Conservative Party was upset at Winston for switching sides. But Winston was an independent thinker.

Despite Winston's busy schedule as a Member of Parliament, he found time to do what he always loved—write. He wrote a biography about his father, Lord Randolph Churchill, that was published in 1906. It was eight hundred and forty pages. His brother, Jack, helped him research the book.

In April 1908, Winston was named president of the Board of Trade in Parliament. This was an important position. He tried to help people who were old, sick, or didn't have jobs.

Winston's writing and political career were thriving, as was his social life. He loved attending dinner parties for the interesting conversation, good food, and fancy drinks like champagne and whiskey. But Winston was shy around women. He did not date much. Part of the reason was that he didn't think of himself as handsome. He was overweight and losing his hair. He was thirty-four years old when he met Clementine Hozier at a party. Clementine also came from a wealthy and respected family. At first, Winston didn't even have the courage to speak to her.

"Winston never uttered a word," said Clementine about the first time she met him. "He just stood and stared."

Despite this awkward beginning, Clementine and Winston fell in love. "Clemmie" loved listening to Winston talk about his work. He valued her support and opinions. They called each other by nicknames. She was his "Cat," and he was her "Pug." They married on September 12, 1908, and remained a perfect match throughout their lives. They sent each other love letters whenever they were apart.

In July 1909, Winston and Clementine's first child, Diana, was born. They had four more children—Randolph, Sarah, Marigold, and Mary—over the next thirteen years. Unlike his own mother and father, Winston loved spending time with his children. He sometimes even gave them their nightly baths.

In 1910, Winston was named Home Secretary of Great Britain. In this job, he focused on helping prisoners in England and improving their lives once they were released. Having been a prisoner himself in South Africa, he could understand what prison life was like. A year later, Winston was named First Lord of the Admiralty, or head of Great Britain's navy. Winston Churchill had no idea what a large role he and the British navy were about play in world affairs.

Chapter 4
The First Great War

The early years of Winston and Clementine's married life with young children were happy ones.

The Churchills lived in the Admiralty House in London. It was the government home for the head of the navy. His brother Jack was also married with children of his own. He worked as a businessman in London. The two families went on vacation and spent a lot of time together.

World War I erupted on June 28, 1914, when a Serbian man assassinated Archduke Franz Ferdinand of Austria and the archduke's wife. The assassin had wanted Serbia to be free from Austro-Hungarian rule. One month later, Austria-Hungary went to war against Serbia.

European countries took sides. Germany, the
Ottoman Empire in Turkey, and eventually Italy
sided with Austria-Hungary. They were called the
Central Powers. Great Britain sided with Serbia,
Russia, and France; they were called the Allied

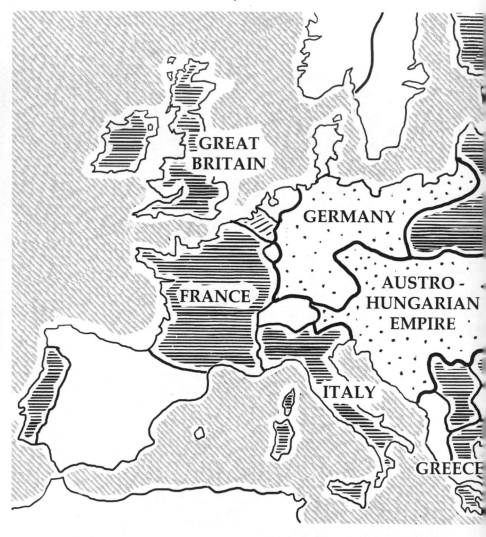

Powers. The United States did not join the Allied Powers until later in the war, in 1917.

Winston loved being in command of the British navy. He loved the excitement of sending ships to fight at sea. Did it make him feel like a child again playing toy soldiers? Perhaps. But Winston's excitement made him too aggressive. In 1915, Winston sent fifteen naval ships on an attack mission near Turkey. The military also sent troops into the Turkish countryside. The Central Powers were prepared to defend the area against the Allied Powers. They gunned down the soldiers who attacked the shoreline and quickly sank three British battleships.

RUSSIAN EMPIRE

TURKEY (OTTOMAN EMPIRE)

Four more ships were soon blown up, and two were disabled. Winston had to call off the rest of the attack.

Winston lost his job as head of the navy. He was sad and shocked because 252,000 Allied soldiers died in the battles on land and at sea.

"I thought he would die of grief," Clementine said about her husband.

Winston still wanted to take part in the war and help his country. He volunteered to join the army to fight on the front lines. He loved being a soldier and was good at it. He was sent to fight in France in November 1915.

Winston served in the military for five and a half months, on the front lines in the trenches. He wrote to his wife asking for supplies such as thigh-high waterproof boots and a sheepskin sleeping bag.

LIFE IN THE TRENCHES

WORLD WAR I WAS A DIRTY AND BRUTAL WAR. THIS WAS THE FIRST WAR THAT SOLDIERS FOUGHT WITH POWERFUL MACHINE GUNS. THE GUNS MADE IT DANGEROUS AND HARD TO ATTACK IN OPEN FIELDS. INSTEAD, BOTH SIDES DUG DEEP TRENCHES AND SHOT AT EACH OTHER FROM BEHIND HIGH WALLS. IF ALL THE TRENCHES WERE LAID END TO END, THEY WOULD HAVE STRETCHED 25,000 MILES. THEY WERE ALL DUG IN MUDDY GROUND AND OFTEN FILLED WITH WATER. RATS WERE EVERYWHERE. GUNFIRE WAS EXCHANGED CONSTANTLY. MANY SOLDIERS ENDED UP WITH LICE IN THEIR HAIR AND SKIN INFECTIONS ON THEIR BODIES. OVER TWO HUNDRED THOUSAND SOLDIERS ARE ESTIMATED TO HAVE DIED IN THE TRENCHES DURING THE WAR.

Clementine and their children were relieved when Winston stopped fighting and returned safely to London.

In 1917, Winston was appointed Minister of Munitions. He was in charge of making sure that enough weapons were sent to the British soldiers. Winston held this position until the war finally came to an end. The Central Powers surrendered

on November 11, 1918.
More than sixteen
million people had
died in the conflict.

World War I was
called the "War to End All
Wars" because no one could imagine such a deadly
and destructive tragedy ever happening again.

Chapter 5
Turning Points

In Great Britain's post-war cabinet, Winston was named Secretary of State for War and Air. He helped bring the troops home and readjust to regular life. The army went from millions of soldiers who served during the war, to just thousands during peacetime. To help make this process smoother, Winston created a policy based on the principle of "first in, first out." If you had been one of the first soldiers to sign up to fight, you were one of the first allowed to go home.

Winston also helped create new boundaries for the countries in the Middle East that had been freed from Turkish rule. The Middle East is the area where Africa, Asia, and Europe meet. In the peace treaty after the war, this land was made into new countries. The Allied Powers who had won the war helped establish Syria, Iraq, and Jordan in the Middle East.

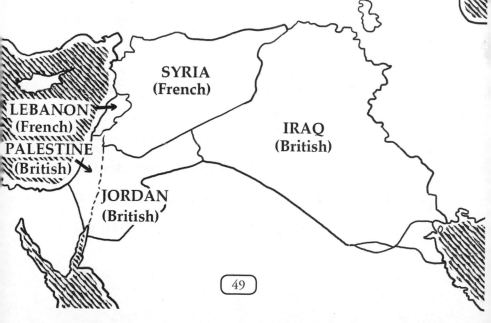

SYRIA
(French)

LEBANON
(French)
PALESTINE
(British)

IRAQ
(British)

JORDAN
(British)

In 1921, Winston took a new cabinet position, Colonial Secretary, where he would continue to work with countries in the Middle East. He also worked with Irish people—called Nationalists—who did not want to be under British rule any more. Winston agreed this was the right thing for Ireland. He helped create a peace treaty that allowed Southern Ireland to become an independent country.

HOME RULE FOR IRELAND

The Right Hon LORD PIRRIE K.P. HML

The Right Hon WINSTON CHURCHILL M.P.

Mr JOHN REDMOND M.P.

Unreserved 1/-

CELTIC PARK FOOTBALL GROUNDS, FEBRUARY 8th, 1912.

This busy time in Winston's life was also a period of personal tragedy. He and his mother had grown close since Winston's father had died.

She was sixty-seven years old when she fell down the stairs and died from her injuries. Shortly afterward, Winston's daughter Marigold died from an infection. She was just shy of three years old. Winston and Clementine sat by Marigold's bedside. They sang her favorite nursery songs to comfort her. They were beyond grief when she died in August that same year. Clementine was so upset that she cried out "like an animal in mortal pain." Winston made visits to Marigold's grave for the rest of his life.

In September 1922, Winston and Clementine had their fifth and final child, Mary. Winston was thrilled. A month later, Winston had to have emergency appendix surgery. It was an election year, and Winston was too sick to campaign. He lost the election.

"In the twinkling of an eye, I found myself without an office, without a seat, without a party, and without an appendix," Winston wrote in an essay.

The Churchills bought a new country home, called Chartwell, in Kent, England.

Without work to occupy his time, Winston dove back into painting, a hobby he had begun before World War I. Painting made him feel peaceful. He took lessons and proved to be a talented artist. Winston was especially good at painting landscapes. He also had more time to write. While on vacation with his family and Jack's family in France, he began writing *The World Crisis,* a six-volume history of World War I.

In 1924, Winston returned to politics. He switched parties once again and rejoined the Conservative side. He was reelected to Parliament and named Chancellor of the Exchequer for Great Britain. This position put him in charge of money matters for his country. It was a strange position for a man who had barely passed his math classes as a boy, but it was the same position his father had once held nearly forty years earlier.

Winston was Chancellor for the next five years.
He wasn't very good at this job. He even called it
the worst office he ever held.

British citizens were unhappy, too. Millions of people were poor and not working. They blamed Winston and the government for their problems. In May of 1929, Winston and the Conservative Party lost the general election. Winston was fifty-five years old. He would not hold another political position for more than ten years. Most people in Great Britain thought his career was over. They were wrong.

Chapter 6
The Wilderness Years

Winston decided to go to the United States on a speaking tour. He was world famous because of his political jobs, and also because of the books he wrote. People loved to hear him speak about World War I.

After the tour ended, Winston went back to England. He spent his time writing and painting in the country at Chartwell. His lifetime love of food and drink endured. He still loved to have guests over for dinner parties.

Winston's children were older by then. They were away at school or living on their own. Winston remained close to all of them. His only son, Randolph, was a writer for a British newspaper. Winston and Randolph disagreed about world issues. They sometimes fought with each other about events of the day, but they always made up.

During the next decade, from 1929 to 1939, Winston wrote eleven books. The books were filled with lively stories about his adventures as a young man. He also wrote about his famous ancestors and more about World War I. He also found time to write hundreds of magazine articles and many speeches for the House of Commons! The articles and speeches were mostly about events of the day. People were interested in Winston's opinions. His books and articles were very popular.

Winston later called this time in his life the "Wilderness Years." He was not at the center of British politics, only writing about it from the outside. But while in the "wilderness," Winston paid close attention to the events unfolding in Germany. World War I had left the defeated country in shambles. The new German leader, Adolf Hitler, hated many different nations and races.

He blamed other people—especially Jewish people— and other countries for Germany's problems.

Winston feared Hitler would start another war. He wrote newspaper and magazine articles that warned people Adolf Hitler was a dangerous man. He thought Hitler wanted to invade Germany's neighbors and rule all of Europe. Churchill wanted Great Britain to begin preparing for another possible war against Germany. Many people didn't take Hitler, or Winston's warnings, seriously. After losing close to a million British soldiers during World War I, they wanted Great Britain to remain at peace. Unfortunately, Winston was soon proven to be right.

THE RISE OF ADOLF HITLER AND THE NAZIS

ADOLF HITLER HAD BEEN A SOLDIER DURING WORLD WAR I. AFTER THE WAR, HE BEGAN TO MAKE SPEECHES PROMISING THINGS WOULD BE BETTER FOR THE GERMAN PEOPLE IF HE BECAME GERMANY'S NEXT LEADER. PEOPLE BELIEVED IN HIM. HE BECAME CHANCELLOR OF GERMANY IN 1933.

ADOLF HITLER

HITLER'S POLITICAL PARTY WAS CALLED THE NAZIS. YOUNG PEOPLE ACROSS GERMANY WERE ENCOURAGED TO SUPPORT HITLER AND HIS PARTY.

THEY JOINED "HITLER YOUTH" CLUBS. HITLER WANTED
TO GET RID OF WHAT HE CONSIDERED "INFERIOR"
RACES, LIKE GYPSIES AND JEWS. HE BUILT UP A
STRONG ARMY. HIS GOAL WAS TO CONQUER
COUNTRIES ALL OVER EUROPE. HE WANTED TO
MAKE GERMANY THE MOST POWERFUL EMPIRE ON
EARTH. THIS EMPIRE WAS CALLED THE THIRD REICH.
HE THOUGHT IT WOULD LAST A THOUSAND YEARS,
BUT IT ONLY LASTED TWELVE.

Chapter 7
Blood, Toil, Tears, and Sweat

In September 1938, the prime minister of Great Britain, Neville Chamberlain, flew to Munich, Germany. Adolf Hitler had broken all his promises and rebuilt an army to invade Austria. But Chamberlain held out hope for peace.

Chamberlain and Hitler signed a document called the Munich Agreement. The agreement allowed Hitler to take control of Czechoslovakia. In return, Hitler promised not to invade other countries. Prime Minister Chamberlain returned to Great Britain a hero. He declared he had "secured peace in our time."

Winston never believed Hitler. He thought the German leader would go back on his word. Winston was right. Only one year later, Germany invaded Poland. Now Great Britain vowed to fight. On September 3, 1939, Great Britain and France declared war on Germany. Prime Minister Chamberlain asked Winston to take his old office as head of the

British navy. A joyful signal was sent out to the British fleets: "Winston is back!"

Neville Chamberlain was not an effective wartime leader. In May 1940, he resigned as prime minster of Great Britain. The nation turned to Winston Churchill. At age sixty-five, Winston took on the most important job of his life. It was the job he had been preparing for since his days at boarding school as a boy. Winston was named the new prime minister of Great Britain.

"I have nothing to offer but blood, toil, tears, and sweat," Winston said in his first speech as prime minister. "Let us go forward together with our united strength."

Members of the House rose to their feet and cheered as loud as they could. They believed in their new leader.

Winston's first month as prime minister was not easy. German troops invaded other countries—Belgium, Holland, and Luxembourg. Great Britain could not stop them. After just six weeks, their only ally, France, surrendered to Germany. Great Britain now stood alone against the Nazis.

Winston made many speeches encouraging the nation. His speeches were broadcast on the radio all over the country. He worked hard to get his words just right.

He often spent one hour preparing for every minute of the speech he was about to give. If a speech was thirty minutes long, he spent nearly thirty hours working on it! But the effort was always worthwhile.

Winston's words gave his people strength and courage. They brought people together. They reminded the British people of their proud history and bright future. They kept soldiers fighting when victory seemed impossible.

"If the British Empire and its commonwealth last for a thousand years, men still will say, 'This was their finest hour,'" Winston said famously.

In the summer of 1940, Germany attacked Great Britain. They dropped bombs on the city of London for fifty-seven nights in a row. People slept in the subway tunnels for safety. London became a city of burned-down buildings. More than one million homes were damaged or destroyed.

Both Winston's and Jack's families moved to the country. But the Churchill brothers remained at Winston's home in London. Winston refused to sleep inside a protected government bunker. Although he spent his nights watching the bombings from the roof of government buildings, he returned to his home afterward. He wanted to endure these attacks in the same way that the British civilians did.

Great Britain's Air Force fought back as hard as they could. More than twenty-three thousand British civilians died in the bombings. Winston walked in the ruins in the days after each bombing and told survivors to stay strong. The British people listened to Winston in person and on the radio. They never gave up or surrendered.

Stalled by England's refusal to quit, and backed by its allies Italy and Japan, Germany ended the blitz and invaded the Soviet Union instead.

RADIO MAKES WAVES

BY THE MID-NINETEENTH CENTURY, GUGLIELMO MARCONI WAS EXPERIMENTING WITH RADIO WAVES. YET, IT WASN'T UNTIL 1940 THAT ALMOST EVERY

GUGLIELMO MARCONI

HOUSE IN AMERICA HAD ONE. PEOPLE ENJOYED MUSIC AND COMEDY SHOWS ON THE RADIO. THEY ALSO RELIED ON IT FOR IMPORTANT NEWS. LEADERS AROUND THE GLOBE BROADCAST THEIR MESSAGES DIRECTLY INTO PEOPLE'S HOMES BY RADIO. PRESIDENT FRANKLIN ROOSEVELT USED RADIO TO COMFORT THE UNITED STATES DURING THE TROUBLED YEARS OF THE 1930S DEPRESSION. HE CALLED HIS TALKS "FIRESIDE CHATS." WINSTON CHURCHILL'S SPEECHES, HOWEVER, WERE MUCH MORE INTENSE, REACHING A WORLDWIDE AUDIENCE DURING WORLD WAR II. HIS BOOMING, GRAVELLY VOICE BOOSTED MORALE AND GAVE THE WORLD HOPE TO "KEEP CALM AND CARRY ON." THIS BRITISH MOTTO IS STILL REPEATED ALL OVER THE WORLD!

In the summer of 1941, Winston met United States President Franklin Roosevelt. The meetings took place in Placentia Bay, Newfoundland, Canada, aboard a British battleship, the *Prince of Wales*. The talks resulted in the Atlantic Charter, in which both leaders pledged to protect the rights of countries in choosing their own government and to live free from fear. Despite this charter, Roosevelt didn't commit the United States to joining the war. He did, however, help the war effort by supplying weapons, food, and other supplies to the Allies.

On December 7, 1941, President Roosevelt's position changed after Japan attacked a US naval base in Pearl Harbor, Hawaii.

The United States declared war on Japan and
Germany. They entered World War II on the side
of Great Britain and the Soviet Union.

Roosevelt told Winston over the phone, "We are all in the same boat now."

Franklin Roosevelt and Winston Churchill continued to be great friends and partners during the war. The president admired Winston's strength and determination. Roosevelt said about Winston, "He's about the greatest man in the world. In fact he may very likely be the greatest."

The Soviet Union, Great Britain, and the United States were now the major Allied Powers fighting the Axis Powers of Germany, Italy, and Japan.

Dozens of other countries also chose sides and sent soldiers to war.

Winston worked eighteen hours a day. He traveled to meet with world leaders. He visited and rallied his troops wherever they were fighting. Newspapers called him "the British Bulldog" and drew cartoons that made him look like one. He was called a bulldog because he was fierce and ready to attack the enemy.

HOLDING THE LINE!

THE HOLOCAUST

ADOLF HITLER BLAMED JEWISH PEOPLE FOR ALL OF GERMANY'S TROUBLES AFTER THE FIRST WORLD WAR. HE THOUGHT JEWISH PEOPLE WEREN'T AS GOOD AS GERMANS. DURING WORLD WAR II, ADOLF HITLER SENT JEWISH PEOPLE AND OTHERS TO CONCENTRATION CAMPS. IN THOSE CAMPS, PEOPLE WERE KILLED BY POISONOUS GAS. OTHERS STARVED TO DEATH OR DIED FROM DISEASES.

THE HOLOCAUST IS ONE OF THE MOST HORRIBLE CRIMES IN HUMAN HISTORY. IN TOTAL, ADOLF HITLER AND THE NAZIS MURDERED SIX MILLION JEWISH PEOPLE. ONE MILLION OF THEM WERE CHILDREN. THE NAZIS MURDERED AS MANY AS SEVENTEEN MILLION INNOCENT PEOPLE, INCLUDING RUSSIAN AND POLISH CITIZENS, CATHOLICS, AND PEOPLE WITH MENTAL AND PHYSICAL DISABILITIES.

When appearing in public, Winston waved
his hand high in the air and made a V sign for
victory. People cheered whenever he flashed the
victory sign.

The tides began to change for the Allied
Powers after the United States joined their side.
In June 1944, the Allied Powers invaded the
northern coast of France and drove the German
forces out. The attack, known as D-Day, was
the beginning of the end for Hitler. Germany
surrendered in April 1945.

Adolf Hitler committed suicide before he could be captured. Only Japan kept fighting. They finally surrendered in August 1945, after the United States dropped atomic bombs on two of its cities.

The war was finally over. More than seventy million people had died in bloody battles, bombings, and horrible crimes against innocent victims.

For some, life would never be the same. But the world was free in part because of Winston Churchill's leadership.

Over the radio, Winston told the British people, "This is your victory! It is the victory of the cause of freedom in every land."

Chapter 8
The Greatest Leader

Just a couple months after the war ended, the British people voted again for prime minister. It was a very hard time. England had no money after the war. Voters thought Winston would pay too much attention to world problems. They wanted a leader who would focus on rebuilding their country. Although Winston was loved and respected around the world, his Conservative Party was voted out.

In 1946, Winston and his wife, Clementine, took a trip to the United States. He was world famous, and the American people admired him. Huge crowds came to hear him wherever he spoke. On March 5, Winston made one of his most famous speeches ever at Westminster College in

Fulton, Missouri. The new US President Harry
Truman was in the audience.

Winston spoke about the growing tension
between the Soviet Union—a communist
country—and democratic nations. Communism
is a system where individuals don't own land
or businesses. Instead, the government owns
everything. After World War II, Germany was
split into two countries. The Soviet Union took

control of countries—including East Germany, Poland, and Czechoslovakia—now freed from the Nazis. They forced communist rule on them. The countries freed by Great Britain and the United States, like West Germany and France, set up democratic governments, which were ruled by elected officials.

Winston did not think communism was a fair system of government. He feared that communist countries would start more wars in an effort to control more of the world. In his speech, Winston warned, "an iron curtain has descended across the Continent [of Europe]."

Winston used "iron curtain" to describe the division that separated the free people in Western Europe from the oppressed people in Eastern Europe. He warned there could be another war because of this divide. In fact, this speech marked the beginning of what became known as the Cold War.

THE COLD WAR (1945–1991)

THE COLD WAR MARKED A PERIOD WHEN SOVIET-LED COMMUNIST COUNTRIES WERE CONSTANTLY ON THE BRINK OF WAR WITH THE UNITED STATES AND ITS ALLIES. BOTH SIDES FEARED THE OTHER WOULD USE ATOMIC WEAPONS.

YET THE COLD WAR WAS NOT AN ACTUAL WAR. INSTEAD, BATTLES UNFOLDED IN "HOT" PLACES LIKE KOREA AND VIETNAM, WHERE THE US TRIED TO STOP THE SPREAD OF COMMUNISM. THE TENSION BETWEEN THE SOVIET UNION AND THE UNITED STATES WAS VIEWED AS A "COLD" STANDOFF.

WHEN MIKHAIL GORBACHEV BECAME THE
SOVIETS' NEW LEADER IN 1985, HE STARTED TO
COOPERATE WITH THE UNITED STATES AND ITS
PRESIDENT, RONALD REAGAN. BY 1989, BOTH
LEADERS HAD SIGNED AGREEMENTS TO REDUCE
THE NUMBER OF BOMBS AND WEAPONS THEY
KEPT. ONCE THE SOVIETS BECAME FRIENDLIER
WITH THE UNITED STATES, THIS FREED ITS
NEIGHBORS TO FORM INDEPENDENT DEMOCRATIC
NATIONS. SOON AFTER, THE SOVIET UNION
COLLAPSED. THE COLD WAR OFFICIALLY ENDED
IN 1991.

During his Missouri speech, Winston also spoke about the United Nations. The United Nations was founded in 1945 at the end of World War II. It is an organization of countries that  have agreed to work together to prevent wars. Members of the UN are supposed to resolve differences between countries with diplomacy, by having discussions about their differences, rather than force. From the fifty-one founding countries, the UN has grown to nearly two hundred.

After the Churchills' trip across the United States, the couple returned to Chartwell. All their kids were grown and had their own children. Winston and Clementine loved spending time and playing with their grandchildren.

Winston began writing *Memoirs of the Second*

World War. The book was more than five thousand pages and helped Churchill to win the Nobel Prize in Literature in 1953. The Nobel Prize is one of the highest honors an author can receive.

"This gives me an opportunity to look back and express my views on some of the major events of the last twelve years," Winston wrote about the book.

In the middle of all this writing, Winston's brother, Jack, died in February 1947. He was sixty-seven years old. Although Jack never worked in politics himself, he always supported Winston. They were close their entire lives, and Winston missed his brother terribly after he died.

In 1951, Winston's Conservative Party regained control of Parliament. Winston was appointed prime minister of Great Britain for the second time. Winston was now seventy-six years old and still devoted to leading his country.

In March 1953, Queen Elizabeth II acknowledged Winston's lifetime of service when she made Winston Churchill a knight. This honor is one of the oldest and highest honors that can be given to a person in Great Britain. Winston was now called Sir Winston.

In 1953, Winston suffered a stroke. Although he recovered, he lost much of his energy. The job of prime minster became too big for him to handle. In April 1955, at age seventy-eight, Winston resigned. His long and amazing career was starting to wind down.

Chapter 9
The Twilight Years

In the last ten years of Winston's life, he was awarded many honors. In 1955, he won the Charlemagne Prize from Germany. This prize is one of the highest honors a world leader can receive. Winston was given the prize for his role of bringing peace back to the world. Winston also

continued to write and paint during these years. His last great book was called *A History of the English-Speaking Peoples* and was published in 1958. Winston once said "history will be kind to me because I intend to write it." He meant it as a joke, but he wrote enough historical books for this to be true!

In 1963, Winston was named an honorary citizen of the United States by President John F. Kennedy. His son, Randolph, and his grandson Winston received the honor for him in Washington, DC. This was a thrilling moment for Sir Winston.

He had always felt a strong connection to the United States.

In October 1963, Winston's daughter Diana died unexpectedly at age fifty-four. Winston's youngest daughter, Mary, broke the terrible news to her father. "He withdrew into a great and distant silence," Mary said about Winston's reaction.

In January 1965, Winston had another stroke. He died on January 24, 1965, the very same day his father had died seventy years earlier. Winston's loving wife, Clemmie, was at his bedside.

Clementine and Winston had ten grandchildren and three great-grandchildren during their time together. They had remained a close and loving family throughout Winston's entire life.

Winston was buried next to his mother and father at a cemetery near Blenheim Palace. Clementine was eventually buried there, too.

The family's palace was the perfect final resting
spot for a man who devoted his life to honoring
his family and serving his country.

Many people still think of Winston Churchill
as one of the greatest leaders who ever lived. He
kept the world hopeful and strong during one of

its darkest times in history. He truly believed that success is not final and failure is not fatal; it is the courage to continue that counts.

THE USS *WINSTON S. CHURCHILL*

TODAY, WINSTON CHURCHILL IS STILL LOVED AND RESPECTED IN THE UNITED STATES AND AROUND THE WORLD. IN 2001, A NEW GUIDED-MISSILE DESTROYER, THE USS *WINSTON S. CHURCHILL*, JOINED THE UNITED STATES NAVY. IT IS THE COUNTRY'S FIRST WARSHIP TO CARRY THE NAME OF A FOREIGN LEADER. THE MOTTO OF THE SHIP IS: "IN WAR: RESOLUTION, IN PEACE: GOODWILL."

TIMELINE OF
WINSTON CHURCHILL'S LIFE

1874 —— Born November 30

1887 —— Enters the world famous all-boys Harrow School

1893 —— Enrolls in the Royal Military Academy, Sandhurst

1904 —— Leaves the Conservative Party to join the Liberal Party

1908 —— Marries Clementine Hozier on September 12

1909 —— First child, Diana, born on July 11

1910 —— Named Home Secretary

1911 —— Named First Lord of the Admiralty
Second child, Randolph, born on May 28

1914 —— Third child, Sarah, born on October 7

1917 —— Appointed Minister for Munitions

1918 —— Fourth child, Marigold, born on November 15

1919 —— Appointed Secretary of State for War and Air

1921 —— Marigold dies on August 23
Acts as Colonial Secretary

1922 —— Mary, Churchill's fifth and final child, born on September 15
Churchill leaves the Liberal Party to join the Conservative
Party again

1924 —— Appointed Chancellor of the Exchequer

1940 —— Becomes Prime Minister of Great Britain

1946 —— Gives "Iron Curtain" speech in Missouri

1951 —— Reelected Prime Minister of Great Britain

1953 —— Wins Nobel Prize for Literature

1965 —— Dies January 24, age ninety

TIMELINE OF
THE WORLD

President James Garfield of the United States dies after being shot	1881
Karl Benz drives the world's first car	1885
Eiffel Tower is unveiled in Paris, France	1889
Wright brothers fly a plane in Kitty Hawk, North Carolina	1903
The *Titanic* sinks on its first voyage on April 14	1912
World War I begins	1914
Russian Revolution begins	1917
World War I ends	1918
Civil War in Ireland; League of Nations forms	1922
Franklin Delano Roosevelt becomes president of the United States Adolf Hitler becomes chancellor of Germany	1933
World War II begins	1939
World War II ends; Cold War begins United Nations replaces League of Nations	1945
British rule in India ends	1947
Elizabeth II becomes Queen of England	1952
Berlin Wall built	1961
Cuban Missile Crisis almost causes war between the United States and the USSR	1962

BIBLIOGRAPHY

Ashworth, Leon. **British History Makers: Winston Churchill**. London: Cherrytree, 2001.

Churchill, Winston. **Memoirs of the Second World War**. Boston: Houghton Mifflin, 1959.

Churchill, Winston. **My Early Life: 1874–1904**. New York: Charles Scribner's Sons, 1930.

Churchill, Winston. **The World Crisis: 1911–1918**. New York: Charles Scribner's Sons, 1931.

Clarke, Peter. **Mr. Churchill's Profession: Statesman, Orator, Writer**. London: Bloomsbury, 2012.

Coombs, David. **Churchill: His Paintings**. Cleveland: World Publishing Company, 1967

Humes, James C. **Churchill: The Prophetic Statesman**. Washington, DC: Regnery History, 2012.

* Books for young readers

Jenkins, Roy. **Churchill**. New York: MacMillan, 2001.

Johnson, Paul. **Churchill**. New York: Viking, 2009.

Keegan, John. **Winston Churchill**. New York: Viking, 2002.

Lee, Celia, and John Lee. **The Churchills: A Family Portrait**. New York: Palgrave McMillian, 2010.

* MacDonald, Fiona. **Winston Churchill**. New York: World Almanac Library, 2003.

Manchester, William. **The Last Lion: Winston Spenser Churchill: Alone, 1932–1940**. New York: Little, Brown, 1988.

Pearson, John. **The Private Lives of Winston Churchill**. London: Bloomsbury, 1991.

* Reynolds, Quentin James. **Winston Churchill**. New York: Random House, 1963.

Sandys, Celia. **From Winston with Love and Kisses: The Young Churchill**. London: Sinclair-Stevenson, 1994.

* Severance, John B. **Winston Churchill: Soldier, Statesman, Artist**. New York: Clarion Books, 1996.

Shelden, Michael. **Young Titan: The Making of Winston Churchill**. New York: Simon & Schuster, 2013.

WEBSITES

Nationalchurchillmuseum.org

Winstonchurchill.org